DYNAMIC DUOS
2014

SCHOLASTIC INC.

PHOTO CREDITS:
Photo Editor: Cynthia Carris

cover, top: Keith Srakocic/AP Images; bottom: Harry E. Walker/MCT/Getty
Images; back cover, top left: Mark Reis/Colorado Springs Gazette/MCT/
Getty Images; top right: Leon Halip/Getty Images; bottom left: Tom Lynn/
AP Images; bottom right: Jeff Gross/Getty Images; interior backgrounds:
Danil Melekhin/iStockphoto; p1, top left: Gregory Shamus/Getty Images;
top right: Laurence Kesterson/Reuters; bottom left: Jack Dempsey/AP
Images; bottom right: Christopher Szagola/Cal Sport Media/Landov; p4,
top: Shannon Stapleton/Reuters; bottom: Damian Strohmeyer/AP Images;
p6: Damian Strohmeyer/AP Images; p7: Christian Petersen/Getty Imag-
es; p8: Kevin C. Cox/Getty Images; p9: Kevin C. Cox/Getty Images; p10,
top: Christian Petersen/Getty Images; bottom: Jim Bryant/UPI/Newscom;
p12: Jeff Gross/Getty Images; p13: Harry How/Getty Images; p14: Elaine
Thompson/AP Images; p15: Harry E. Walker/MCT/Getty Images; p16, top:
Rick Osentoski/AP Images; bottom: Leon Halip/Getty Images; p18: Tannen
Maury/EPA/Newscom; p19: Jose Juarez/AP Images; p20: Leon Halip/Getty
Images; p21: Gregory Shamus/Getty Images; p22, top: Paul Jasienski/AP
Images; bottom: Andy Lyons/Getty Images; p24: David Welker/Getty Im-
ages; p25: Ric Tapia/AP Images; p26, top: Kevin Terrell/AP Images; bottom:
Jonathan Daniel/Getty Images; p27: Ray Carlin/Icon SMI/Newscom; p28:
Wesley Hitt/Getty Images; p29: Damon Tarver/Cal Sport Media/Newscom;
p30: Jeff Gross/Getty Images; p31: Rich Kane/Icon SMI/Corbis.

No part of this publication may be reproduced, stored in a retrieval system, or transmitted in any
form or by any means, electronic, mechanical, photocopying, recording, or otherwise, without
written permission of the publisher. For information regarding permission, write to Scholastic Inc.,
Attention: Permissions Department, 557 Broadway, New York, NY 10012.

978-0-545-72218-6

Published by Scholastic Inc.
SCHOLASTIC and associated logos are trademarks and/or registered trademarks of Scholastic Inc.

12 11 10 9 8 7 6 5 4 3 2 1   14 15 16 17 18 19/0

Designed by Cheung Tai
Printed in the U.S.A.   40
First printing, September 2014

CONTENTS

INTRODUCTION

You can't play football alone. Well, you can, but it's not as much fun. So it's a good thing that part of being on a team means having great teammates. They play with and for one another. They win and lose together, helping one another along the way. These are pairs of teammates who combine their individual skills to make their teams into winners. Playing together is the key to their success.

PEYTON MANNING
AND
WES WELKER

Without a quarterback, receivers can't do their jobs. Without receivers, all a quarterback can do is hand the ball off . . . or run. The relationship between a QB and his pass-catchers is vital to a successful team. In 2013, no NFL QB had a better connection with his receivers than Peyton Manning of the Denver Broncos. Manning, already an NFL superstar, surpassed even himself. He set new single-season records with 55 touchdown passes and 5,477 passing yards. Though his team lost in Super Bowl XLVIII, he won his all-time record fifth NFL MVP award.

But he would not have set any of those marks without receivers such as Wes Welker. The veteran receiver joined the Broncos for the 2013 season after six seasons (and five Pro Bowls) with New England. He had been Patriots quarterback Tom Brady's favorite target. Welker brought veteran leadership to a young receiving group for Denver. In his first season playing with Manning, Welker had 73 catches—10 of those went for touchdowns.

Those 10 touchdowns to Welker were part of Manning's record season. In fact, Welker joined teammates Demaryius Thomas, Julius Thomas, Eric Decker, and Knowshon Moreno with at least 10 TDs. The Broncos were the first team in NFL history to have five players score that many TDs in a single season—four of those players, of course, depended on passes from Manning to reach the end zone. (Moreno is a running back, but three of his scores came via passes.) Welker and the entire Denver offense were excited to be at the receiving end of history!

As a QB, Manning's great skill is reading defenses.

He often makes changes at the line of scrimmage, directing his receivers to new routes. The only way that strategy works is if he has excellent and smart receivers. Welker fits that bill perfectly. He led the NFL in catches in 2007, 2009, and 2011. He's an expert at turning a short catch into a long gain. As he had done with Brady, Welker became the perfect across-the-middle pass-catcher for Manning. (Just don't ask Welker to pick which of his future Hall of Fame teammates he likes better!)

With the Broncos, Welker's Denver teammates Demaryius Thomas and Decker did most of the deep work downfield. That meant that Welker and Manning could take advantage of the space those guys created to work their magic together. Welker is only 5'9", pretty small for a receiver in today's NFL.

MANNING ON WELKER:

"As a quarterback, when you get a receiver who [works as hard as Wes does], I mean, that gets you pumped up about football."

WELKER on MANNING:

"The balls are just so accurate and you come out of your break and the ball is just there. It's almost like a long handoff sometimes. He definitely makes it easy on you."

But his speed and ability to run perfect routes have made him a star. Those skills connect perfectly with Manning's ability to zing perfect passes and to find weaknesses in the defense.

This touchdown twosome got off to a fast start. In the first game that Welker played with Manning, he caught two of Manning's NFL-record-tying seven TD passes. In that same game, he had a season-high nine receptions. Welker snagged two more TDs in a rout of Philadelphia a few weeks later. In a key AFC West showdown against the Kansas City Chiefs late

in the season, Welker caught eight passes from Manning, and the Broncos sealed the division title. In fact, Welker caught at least three passes in every game in the 2013 season.

The duo kept the ball rolling, or . . . flying, in the playoffs. Against San Diego, Manning threw a key touchdown pass to Welker on the way to a win. Against Welker's old team, the Patriots, in the AFC Championship Game, the receiver suffered a concussion and missed most of the game (but he still had four catches). In the Super Bowl, even eight Manning-to-Welker connections were not enough to stop the Seattle blowout.

But Manning and Welker have both been there before. Manning has lost one Super Bowl (though he did win one, too), while Welker has now lost three. These veterans know that once training camp starts, they'll be teaming up to try to get the Broncos back to the top . . . together.

DYNAMIC DUO DIGEST

MANNING		WELKER
6'5"	HEIGHT	5'9"
230	WEIGHT	185
QB	POSITION	WR
TENNESSEE	SCHOOL	TEXAS TECH
1998	FIRST NFL SEASON	2004
1	SEASONS TOGETHER	1

TEAMMATES FROM HISTORY

Johnny Unitas and Raymond Berry, Colts:
Like Welker, Berry was a student of the game. He ran precise routes and always looked for the open spot. Like Manning, Unitas called his own plays and had a strong, powerful arm. Together, they won a pair of NFL titles and they're both in the Hall of Fame.

RUSSELL WILSON
AND
MARSHAWN LYNCH

NFL players all have long roads to reach the top. They practice and play hard for years and wait for the big break and the right situation. They never do it alone, however. They need teammates to support them and help them win. In Seattle, the Seahawks have a one-two punch on offense that took them all the way to the top—a Super Bowl XLVIII championship!

Quarterback Russell Wilson is the field general for the Seahawks, and his number one weapon is running back Marshawn Lynch. While other NFL teams have gone pass-happy, the Seahawks depend on a strong running game. Wilson makes the throws he needs to, but Lynch is the power behind the NFL's reigning champions.

But both players ended up together at the top after very different roads.

> ## SEAHAWKS COACH PETE CARROLL ON LYNCH:
> "[Marshawn's] attention to taking care of himself is a sign of how committed he is to his teammates and to the team. His consistency is the best thing about him."

In college, Russell Wilson started out at North Carolina State. He did well but felt that it was not the right situation for him. For his senior season in 2011, he transferred to Wisconsin. There he helped the Badgers win the Big Ten Conference and a spot in the Rose Bowl.

The following spring, however, when Wilson was in the NFL Draft, few thought that he would be wearing a Super Bowl ring in 2014. In a draft stocked with great passers, Wilson was the sixth one chosen. Big names like

SEAHAWKS COACH PETE CARROLL ON WILSON:

"He's an extraordinary individual. It goes way beyond his football ability, he's an amazing person. We're just blessed that he's spending his time with us right now. The leadership, the discipline, the hard work, the competitiveness, the toughness that he has and demonstrates, and his uncanny ability to rise to the moment."

Andrew Luck, Robert Griffin III, Ryan Tannehill, and others all went before Seattle chose Wilson.

"I knew that the Seattle Seahawks were going to pick me. I was going to make the other 31 teams regret it," Wilson said.

Wilson's first job was just to earn the starting spot. The same year they drafted Wilson, the Seahawks had signed Matt Flynn from the Packers to a big free-agent contract. They expected Flynn to start and Wilson to back him up. Wilson had other ideas. He excelled in training camp. He impressed coach Pete Carroll so much that Carroll had no choice. Wilson was the starting QB in his first NFL game. It proved to be the right call. Wilson and the Seahawks won 11 games in 2012, four more than in 2011.

Wilson outdid nearly all the great rookie QBs that season, leading the Seahawks to the playoffs. In fact, Wilson's 52 TD passes in his first two seasons are tied for the second-most all time, behind Dan Marino's 68 in 1983–84. Wilson is the only QB ever to win 23 games in his first two seasons.

Meanwhile, Lynch had his own bumpy path to stardom. He was the first-round pick of the Buffalo Bills in 2007 and quickly became a solid player, topping 1,000 yards in each of his first two seasons. But then the Bills soured on him and he played less and less. They traded him to Seattle during the 2010 season. In the Northwest, Lynch thrived. In 2011, he ran for 1,204 yards and a new career-high 12 touchdowns. Lynch's pounding running style earned him a great nickname—Beast Mode! But Seattle only won seven games.

That all changed when Wilson arrived in 2012. Now the Seahawks had a passing game to go with Lynch's running skills. They had a leader to direct the offense. Also, Wilson is very comfortable talking to the media and answering questions. Lynch is very shy and would prefer never to do interviews. Wilson became the face of the team. Meanwhile, Beast Mode kept churning out scores and yards. In fact, he even got help from his QB for some of them. In their

first playoff game against Washington after the 2012 season, Wilson was the lead blocker on Lynch's 27-yard touchdown run! After Wilson arrived, Lynch set a career high with 1,590 yards.

In 2013, the duo, along with a powerful Seattle defense, were at the top of the NFC. With Wilson throwing and Lynch running (and the Seattle D lowering the boom!), the Seahawks won the NFC. In Super Bowl XLVIII, they crushed the Broncos in the Super Bowl, 43–8. Wilson threw for two touchdowns, while Lynch ran for another. Now the teammates have something else to share beside the stories of how they arrived in Seattle: Now they each have a Super Bowl ring!

DYNAMIC DUO DIGEST

WILSON		LYNCH
5'11"	HEIGHT	5'11"
206	WEIGHT	215
QB	POSITION	RB
WISCONSIN	SCHOOL	CALIFORNIA
2012	FIRST NFL SEASON	2007
2	SEASONS TOGETHER	2

TEAMMATES FROM HISTORY

Troy Aikman and Emmitt Smith, Cowboys:
Like Wilson, Aikman had a strong, accurate arm and could make the big play when needed. He relied on the powerful running of Smith, who would end up as the NFL's all-time career rushing leader.

MATT STAFFORD
AND
CALVIN JOHNSON

Sometimes a teammate twosome has one player who gets all the headlines. But both players know that that attention wouldn't happen without great teamwork. That's the case in Detroit, where wide receiver Calvin "Megatron" Johnson is becoming one of the all-time best but every big play he makes starts with quarterback Matthew Stafford. And it's not surprising that with such a skilled pair, the Lions are one of the most pass-happy teams in the NFL.

JOHNSON ON STAFFORD:

"It's fun for me to watch him, just how he throws the ball, how he's moving in the pocket, how he's just making plays . . . how he's making smart plays."

Johnson was no surprise NFL star. Since high school in Georgia, he had been hauling in tons of passes and winning awards. He was heavily recruited by the top schools in the nation. In the end, he chose Georgia Tech so his nearby family could see him play. It turned out they saw a lot of great football! In Johnson's first season at Tech, he was the Rookie of the Year in the Atlantic Coast Conference. He was All-American as a sophomore, and as a junior won the Biletnikoff Award as the top receiver in the nation. Then it was on to the NFL.

He was chosen number three overall by the Lions in 2007. As good as Johnson was, however, and even though he led the NFL with twelve touchdown catches in 2008, the Lions were, um . . . not good. They became the first NFL team to lose all 16 games in one season.

The Lions knew they needed someone to lead their

team and to get Johnson the ball more often. They needed a passer, and they found what they needed in strong-armed Matthew Stafford.

Stafford was a Texas high school All-American, helping his team win a state title. At the University of Georgia, he showed off a powerful arm that had NFL written all over it. He starred with the Bulldogs for three seasons and then turned to the NFL. He was chosen by the Lions first overall in 2009, signing a contract that guaranteed him more than $40 million, the highest ever to that point.

For their first two seasons, Stafford and Johnson clicked a bit but did not fire on all cylinders. The team had no running game and a poor defense. Plus, Stafford missed several games in 2010 with injuries. In fact, the Lions won only six games during the duo's first two seasons on the team.

STAFFORD ON JOHNSON:

"The more he catches the ball, the more yards he gets, the better our team is. So when Calvin Johnson catches the ball for us, good things happen. It's been fun to be part of helping him set those records, too."

In 2011, however, they got on the same page in a big way. They started the season hot: Johnson became the first player ever with two or more TD catches in each of this team's first four games. They stayed hot all season, too. Johnson led the NFL with 1,681 receiving yards, while Stafford's 633 pass attempts were the most in the league (and fifth most all-time for a season). More important, the Lions improved to 10–6 and made the playoffs for the first time since 1999. With 5,038 passing yards, Stafford also set a new all-time Lions record; pretty good for a team that had been playing since 1930!

In 2012, the fireworks continued. Stafford and Johnson lit up the NFL and rewrote the record book. Johnson racked up 1,964 receiving yards, breaking a record set by the great Jerry Rice in 1995. Stafford got his own record, attempting

727 passes to break a record set by Drew Bledsoe in 1994. He also led the NFL in completions.

In 2013, Johnson had to miss a couple of games due to injury, so his numbers were down a bit. He didn't miss the game against Dallas in Week 8, however. With Stafford on fire and Johnson running wild, Megatron racked up 329 receiving yards, the second-highest single-game total ever. Stafford showed his big-game leadership at the end of that contest. After a catch by Johnson brought the ball to the one-yard line, Stafford surprised everyone by leaping over the pile into the end zone for the game-winning score!

Through his first 50 games in the NFL, Stafford has more passing yards and completions than any passer in league history and he'd be the first to tell you he could not have done that alone. Calvin Johnson is considered the best at his position in the league, the uncoverable Megatron, but he can't do anything without Stafford getting him the ball.

DYNAMIC DUO DIGEST

STAFFORD		JOHNSON
6'3"	HEIGHT	6'5"
232	WEIGHT	236
QB	POSITION	WR
GEORGIA	SCHOOL	GEORGIA TECH
2009	FIRST NFL SEASON	2007
5	SEASONS TOGETHER	5

TEAMMATES FROM HISTORY

Steve Young and Jerry Rice, 49ers:

While Rice made a lot of his record-setting catches with Joe Montana, Young had a stronger arm, like Stafford. Like Rice, Johnson could catch any kind of ball, short or deep. Rice was going to get the ball—everyone knew it—but no one could stop him.

JAMAAL CHARLES
AND
ALEX SMITH

Sometimes teammates have been together for a while. Other times, great matchups happen almost overnight. That's the case in Kansas City, where running back Jamaal Charles was just waiting for quarterback Alex Smith to come along.

After scoring 36 touchdowns in three college seasons at Texas, Charles joined Kansas City as a third-round draft pick in 2008. By 2009, Charles had become one of the top runners in the AFC. He has at least 1,100 yards in each season since (except 2011, when he was injured). His career average of 5.6 yards per carry is highest ever among running backs . . . all-time! And though he busted out in 2012 for 1,509 yards, he was still not happy. The main reason was that his Chiefs were at the bottom of the AFC West division. They won only two games in 2012.

In 2013, however, things changed. First, new coach Andy Reid came over from the Eagles to reenergize Kansas City. Second, Charles got a new passing partner, Alex Smith. Smith had been a star passer in college at Utah. But he had had a frustrating pro career before joining the Chiefs. Drafted by the 49ers as the first overall pick in 2005, he split time with other passers most of his first six seasons. In 2011, however, he was handed the job full-time and responded by leading the Niners to 13 wins and a spot in the NFC Championship Game. Smith looked liked he had a bright future in the Bay Area . . . finally. Then, midway through a winning 2012 season, the Niners sat Smith down and installed Colin Kaepernick as their QB. Smith was stunned. He had worked hard to earn the top spot and had succeeded when he got it.

In 2013, he got new life when he moved to Kansas City. And waiting for him there was Charles, his new partner in points. Their first season together got off to a flying start, as Kansas City won its first nine games. Charles was moving the chains and breaking off big runs with his high-stepping style. He would end up leading the NFL in touchdowns with 19. Twelve came on the ground, tying him for the NFL lead in that stat, too. The other seven came from—that's right—passes from Smith, including four in one win over Oakland. Meanwhile, Smith set career highs in attempts, completions, passing yards, and passing TDs. He also made his first Pro Bowl.

Though Kansas City lost in the 2013 playoffs, this might be the Midwest match made in heaven—a running back looking for an offensive leader, and a quarterback looking for a chance.

DYNAMIC DUO DIGEST

SMITH		CHARLES
6'4"	HEIGHT	5'11"
217	WEIGHT	199
QB	POSITION	RB
UTAH	SCHOOL	TEXAS
2005	FIRST NFL SEASON	2008
1	SEASONS TOGETHER	1

TEAMMATES FROM HISTORY

New Chiefs / Old Chiefs:

Steady and reliable like Smith, quarterback Len Dawson led Kansas City to a pair of American Football League titles and a win in Super Bowl IV. His partner for the first of those was running back Mike Garrett, a speedy, nifty runner with, like Charles, a basket of moves.

A.J. HAWK
AND
CLAY MATTHEWS

T ime to pick a pair of Packers! Green Bay has a long tradition of outstanding defensive players. In the 1960s, when they won five NFL titles, they boasted a half dozen Hall of Famers making tackles. Two current Packers linebackers carry on that tradition. A.J. Hawk and Clay Matthews each have a role to play, and they play them to perfection.

Hawk is the veteran leader. In college, he helped Ohio State win a national title when he was only a freshman. By the time he was a senior, he was the Lombardi Award winner as the nation's top lineman or linebacker. Drafted fifth overall in 2006, he became a starter right away. How dependable is he? In the eight seasons he has been with Green Bay, he has missed only two games. And that's while playing one of the hardest hitting positions in sports!

For the Packers, Hawk is the defensive quarterback. He gets the calls from the defensive coaches and tells his teammates. He focuses on run support, closing lanes, and stopping ball carriers.

Matthews, his partner on D, has a different role. While he'll happily snag any ballcarriers that come by, his main target is the quarterback. He's been knocking down passers since joining the Packers as their first-round draft pick in 2009. Matthews has racked up 50 sacks in those five seasons, along with four Pro Bowl selections.

Matthews is actually Clay III. He's following a family football tradition. His grandfather, father, and uncle were long-time NFL players. Clay Sr. and Clay Jr. were also both defensive players, too. Uncle Bruce played on the offensive line for nineteen Hall of Fame seasons.

When Matthews joined Hawk and the Pack in '09, he helped add to the team's winning history. By 2010, with Hawk calling the shots and Matthews making them, the Packers returned to the Super Bowl. Matthews won several defensive player of the year awards, and had a career-high 13.5 sacks. He added 3.5 more in the postseason. They celebrated together when the Packers won their thirteenth NFL championship, beating Pittsburgh in Super Bowl XLV.

Since then, the Packers have made the playoffs three more times, struggling in 2013 when star QB Aaron Rodgers missed seven games with a shoulder injury. Hawk and Matthews continue in their roles—Hawk leading his men in the trenches, Matthews flying around looking for someone to tackle. Offensive players connect by passing the ball but these two guys connect on the field, too—when they're smacking into the guy with the ball!

DYNAMIC DUO DIGEST

HAWK		MATTHEWS
6'1"	HEIGHT	6'3"
247	WEIGHT	255
LB	POSITION	LB
OHIO STATE	SCHOOL	USC
2006	FIRST NFL SEASON	2009
5	SEASONS TOGETHER	5

TEAMMATES FROM HISTORY

Back to the Pack:

Linebacker Ray Nitschke and defensive end Willie Davis were
part of all five of the Packers NFL titles in the 1960s. Nitschke
was the fear-inspiring monster, while Davis made sure
quarterbacks didn't wander. Both are in the Hall of Fame.

THE LEGION OF BOOM

Our final teammates aren't just a pair, they're a big group. For the 2013 season, the Seattle Seahawks gathered together a hard-hitting secondary. They were the key players on one of the league's best defenses, allowing a league-low 14.4 points per game. Led by the talkative cornerback Richard Sherman, this group came to be known as the Legion of Boom!

Sherman gets most of the headlines. Not only is he an outstanding cover corner (he led the NFL with eight interceptions in 2013), he has no problem letting everyone know about it. In the NFC Championship Game, he made a game-saving block of a pass that was headed to San

Francisco's Michael Crabtree in the end zone. Sherman got excited after the game while talking about the play. But the fact is, he did make the play and the Seahawks went on to win the Super Bowl two weeks later.

The group got its nickname from fans after hard-hitting strong safety Kam Chancellor said that as a group they "bring the boom." Chancellor has such a rep for hard hits that receivers often avoid his side of the field. Free safety Earl Thomas is the other key member. His specialty is being the last line of defense, the final wall to stop big downfield plays. Byron Maxwell and Walter Thurmond also played key roles in the Legion coming off the bench.

The biggest boom the Legion put together came in Super Bowl XLVIII. They completely shut down the record-setting Peyton Manning. After throwing 55 TDs in the regular season, Manning managed only one in this game and it came late, after the game was decided. Boom, boom, boom indeed!

Defenses or defensive units have a long history of great nicknames. In honor of the Legion of Boom, here's our list of the all-time best.

1960s and 1970s Minnesota Vikings	Purple People Eaters
1960s Los Angeles Rams	Fearsome Foursome
1970s Miami Dolphins	No-Name Defense
1970s Pittsburgh Steelers	Steel Curtain
1960s and 1970s Dallas Cowboys	Doomsday Defense
1970s Denver Broncos	Orange Crush
1977 Atlanta Falcons	Grits Blitz
1940s and 1980s Chicago Bears	Monsters of the Midway
1990s Pittsburgh Steelers	Blitzburgh